GRANDPA JOHN

World War II

As told by John E. O'Hara

Enjoy
John's story
Ray Wolf

John E. O'Hara
National State Representative, **SHL**
Testifying before the Massachusetts General Court – 4th Bristol District
On Massachusetts Silver Haired Legislature - 1987

On the cover: This image is the left half of the sunrise photograph taken by John E. O'Hara. By abutting this book to the left of *Shirley, His Only Love* it will give the complete image. John is pictured in the Navy at 21.

GRANDPA JOHN REMEMBERS

World War II
As told by John E. O'Hara

Raymond A. Wolf

W O L F
PUBLISHING

ISBN – 13: 978-1-5151-7976-4
ISBN – 10: 1515179761

Published by Wolf Publishing
Hope, Rhode Island

Printed in the United States of America

For all general information:
E-mail: theewolf@cox.net

For orders:

Visit us on the Internet at: www.raywolfbooks.com

To my Mom: Helen O. Larson
&
Shirley's Only Love: John E. O'Hara

Two Great Story Tellers
Who told Their Stories in Rhyme

Contents

Acknowledgments

I would like to thank Cecilia A. St. Jean of the Pawtuxet Valley Preservation and Historical Society for suggesting I do a book about John E. O'Hara and his World War II experiences.

I give a great big thank you to John for sharing his most personal stories, poems, and photographs with me to create this book.

Again, thank you Jennifer Carnevale, for editing my fourteenth book.

Unless otherwise noted, all images are courtesy of the National Archives and Records Administration.

Introduction

World War II is an accounting of what John E. O'Hara went through during the war years. John had joined the Civilian Conservation Corp (CCC) program in 1939. He was assigned to the Burlingame Reservation Camp in Charlestown, Rhode Island. Many of the guys from the CCC camp had joined the Marines but his father refused to sign. Then on 7 December, 1941 the Japanese bombed Pearl Harbor. Early one morning in 1942 he boarded a bus in North Providence and headed to the Navy induction center in Providence. After training at Newport's Coddington Point Boot Camp, he was sent by train to Norfolk, Virginia and assigned to the USS William P. Biddle. It was an attack transport. He attended Gray Marine Diesel School and was made an Amphibian Engineer.

John explains: "I wrote my first poem, *Blue Beach*, of my experience in WW II, to help me get over what happened there. After a sea battle, to get out from under the tremendous pressure of battle, guys would do all sorts of things to unwind. Some would sleep, some would play cards, some would exercise, and some would make music.

I found writing poetry about what had happened and the times that I was in, helped me a lot. That is what many of the following poems are about. The lines I put down then and there, after a battle, to help me unwind and to set out what happened that was significant to me.

Blue Beach 2 was the first action I was fired upon. The Messerscmitt sprayed the beach and landing craft with machine gun bullets. The four of us were sitting ducks. It was the only time in my life I was so scared, due to the shock of being defenseless. The movies show soldiers in battle with no fear. That is a lot of bull; you cannot help but be afraid."

John will take you through battles of the war. He shares his most inner thoughts beginning with the *The Triple C* in June 1939 and ending with *The Ghosts of Bataan* in January 1947.

The author wishes to share the following poem with his readers. It was written by his mother, Helen O. Larson. He believes it is appropriate to close the introduction of Grandpa John Remembers: *World War II*.

Lest We Forget

When the 4th of July comes, please don't march and shout with joy
But think of the disabled veterans that went to war when but a boy

When you wave your flag of freedom, let tears fall from your eyes
For the boys who didn't come home, lay in a grave beneath the skies

Think of the mothers, wives and children, that were left with a broken
heart
Some didn't return home because they did their part

Don't you know they faced the enemy with all the courage they had
Don't you know that many were just a lad

Many of them are paralyzed, don't you know or don't you care
They're with a broken heart, day after day just laying there

They fought for our freedom; they were the bravest of men
Please take time to visit them if you possibly can

And as you lay a wreath on their graves this day
Don't be ashamed to shed some tears and please take a moment to pray

June 1986 – Age 75

Dedicated to all the men that were crippled
and laid down their lives for our freedom

Helen O. Larson

One

1939 - 1940

The Civilian Conservation Corps

This is the dynamite crew at the CCC Burlingame Reservation Camp.
18 year old John is sitting on a box that is labeled Atlas Powder Co.
Charlestown, Rhode Island, United States - 1939.
(Courtesy of John E. O'Hara)

The Triple C
June 1939

A product of The Great Depression
Full of doubts and wanderlust
Work was scarce but not the hunger
There was a path we could trust

From civilian habits to army life
Relieving depression opened wide
Like a new novel
Discovering life's newborn pride

The Civilian Conservation Corps
Proved a beacon in our plight
Outdoor work, building muscles
The triple C was so right

Not quite dawn, half awake
Air alive with the revelry sound
Front the chow line to a patrol
Picking butts from the ground

Clearing wetlands
Beach improvements are suddenly a movement
Much faster than lightning
Laser slivered a long Texas Blue Racer

The chow was filling, as for the pay
We made a total of a dollar a day
Thirty dollars a monthly nest
Twenty-two went home, we kept the rest

Singeing hair, smoke filled skies
Pulaski tools, burning eyes
Fighting fires till daylight fades
A special task, a fire brigade

A mound of potatoes is what I see
A drudgery assignment called KP
A thin sharp knife peeling spuds
Another nick, a spot of blood

Dress clothes were issued
A mid-summer night's dream
My pants, coat, tie, and hat
All were colored forest green

The CCC camp now just a memory
A special era from the past
We learned to live and to share
That type of lesson always lasts

John at 18, he had just joined the CCC.
(Courtesy of John E. O'Hara)

Two

1941

Japanese Bomb Pearl Harbor
Burning battleships: Arizona, West Virginia and Tennessee
at Pearl Harbor, US Territory of Hawaii
7 December, 1941

Awakening America Style
December 1941

A sunny Sunday morning in forty-one
December 7th to be exact
An entire nation, dazed and shocked
Pearl Harbor under sneak attack

People filled with mixed emotions
Adrenalin mixed with anger, fright
A cry from our young men of America
"We're determined, we must fight"

Diving down like hungry vultures
Through Hawaii's clouds in the sky
An attack so devious and vile
On that Sunday morn, innocent people die

Blinded by a quest for power
They brazenly showed their might
They underestimated the American Spirit
That will rise again to fight

Young men in every city and state
Will answer America's liberty call
Flooding all recruiting stations
Young men of all stature, both short and tall

After years of being immersed in an isolation mist
America is now wide awake
Our feelings for our nation, our love for liberty
Will prove Japan made a mistake

Three

1942

Henrietta McCormick Hill, wife of Alabama senator Lister Hill,
christening battleship Alabama at Norfolk Naval Shipyard
Portsmouth, Virginia, United States – 16 February, 1942
John would be assigned to the Alabama in October 1942.

Baptism of Fire
1942

The military's raw recruits
With rigid training every day
Prepare for that traumatic moment
The run into harm's way

It will take that first encounter
To take that one step higher
Absolve that first battle feeling
To experience a baptism of fire

Untested recruits man their stations
A cold chill down their spine
Legs of cement, a stomach on fire
For pampering there is no time

Tracers cut through darkened skies
A plane is hit, a falling glow
The new recruits stare in awe
As adrenalin and anxiety grow

The PA sounds, "Secure all stations"
Their self confidence now high
They've finally passed the hardest test
Their initial baptism of fire

The Angry Atlantic Waters
July 1942

Choppy, restless waves of dark gray
Heave and break a shade of green
Bursting white with a vengeful roar
Attacking rocks with foam so clean

The Atlantic Ocean, a wild wilderness
With intruding waves, a vacant crest
That constantly swirls the beaches
Rushing forward then ebbing to rest

A loud, yet scintillating rhythm
A monotonous, fascinating sound
A sea melody of briny waves
Reaching out to gnaw the ground

Watching from a high sea mound
Tumultuous waves dance in exultation
My lost feelings mixed in apprehension
Eyes stare wildly in fascination

Depression Years

November 1942

The mentality of those Depression years
When class was blended into one
The trademark of the family father
Then passed on to the eldest son

Depression years, an emotional burden
Oh, if only it was in the past
People prayed for God's intervention
"How long will this Depression last?"

They looked to Heaven for a holy visitation
To relieve their pain, release their tension
Employment was scarce and hard to find
Retarding the young people's expectations

A virus invaded our class society
To protect our retreating existence
From sheer fear and desperation
And it became the people's top priority

Dreams of rising beyond their caste
No longer nurtured the youth's mind
Through desperation and high unemployment
Many desperate people turned to crime

Moments Before
November 1942

Those moments before the action starts
An inner battle then takes place
Your mouth is dry, stomach turns cold
Suddenly your heart begins to race

A strange interaction of fear and loyalty
Conflicting reasoning of life and death
A moment of truth invades the mind
Fighting to control my intense inner stress

Robert Feller
Posing before a 40 MM Bofors Quad
Feller was transferred to the Great Lakes
O'Hara was his replacement.

USS William P. Biddle (AP-15)
September 1942

Prelude to Operation Torch
November 1942

Boot Camp training now completed
Young recruits herded on trains
Wonder where this train is headed
Many asked, the weary complained

Our destination, no answers forthcoming
This was the order of the day
Yet, there is one thing that's certain
The final stop, still far away

Our destination was an attack transport
USS William P. Biddle by name
Amphibian craft landing training
Was the Navy's priority aim

Little Creek's sandy beach training
We're learning Judo, Asian art
That will provide our self defense
With that much needed extra spark

Some of the landing craft sailors
Now called Amphibian Engineers
Line up at the ship's rope ladder
Until their motor launch appears

Up the choppy, misty James River
To the Gray Marine Diesel School
Learning all about marine diesels
And the use of mechanical tools

Amphibious training now completed
Our next transfer came through
Back on trains to New York City docks
To the famous Pier Ninety-Two

The USS Hugh L. Scott (AP 43)
Now our Amphibian crew's new quarters
Weighing anchor, back to Hampton Roads
Through angry Atlantic waters

A hundred and two group attack transports
Sail out of Chesapeake Bay
The early misty hours before dawn
Anchor hoisted, task force underway

A strange feeling of anticipation
What is happening is not clear
Neither sailors nor soldiers realize
Operation Torch is very near

General George Patton (far left)
With Rear Admiral H. Kent Hewitt

Aboard the USS Augusta off North Africa
November 1942

Blue Beach Two

November 1942

Both Roosevelt and Churchill
Endorsed a strategic plan
An amphibious landing
On French Moroccan land

Nineteen hundred forty-two
November the eighth to be exact
Amphibian forces, "Torch" by name
Their move a historical fact

We're up before dawn
Though I'm still not quite awake
Our landing crafts in the water
Our mission at stake

The dark African skies
Deep with bright stars
Our landing craft motors
Roar like fast racing cars

Some enemy searchlights
Start searching the skies
Looking for high-flying bombers
But none did arrive

A sudden warm land breeze
With an odor of earth
Floats over the task force
And over our berth

Morning dawn is still sleeping
But starting to wake
A faint glow appears
In the East as dawn breaks

The task force of
Operation Brushwood shows
Darkened ships' silhouettes
Against dawn's glow

The landing craft personnel
Come along side
As soon as they're loaded
They will sail with the tide

Down the rope ladder
Soldiers, guns and full packs
General George Patton's
9th Infantry are ready to act

In their eyes anticipation
A fear of the unknown
On each soldier's face not a smile
Not even a grin

A blanket of silence has
Now set the tone
But the strong feeling of brotherhood
No soldier's alone

Around the Hugh L. Scott
Past the Joseph Hewes
The Tasker Bliss's outline
Comes into view

Cruisers Augusta and Brooklyn
Steam into position
Fedhala's the Sherki
The cruiser's target and mission

Fedhala's coastal defense batteries
Nickname it the Sherki
But men in our craft
Renamed it the Turkey

Adrenalin and anticipation
Rush throughout our veins
Our invasion forces are within
Shore batteries range

An explosion off starboard
Bodies blown into the sky
Thoughts of morbid reality
As many young men die

The guns of the Brooklyn
Silence Sherki's site
As on shore our allied paratroopers
Finish the fight

Our landing craft hits the beach
The soldiers on land
Running hard for cover
According to their plans

Our diesel motor has stalled
Which is a bad sign
Around the craft's propeller
Line is entwined

The craft's engineer with a knife
Leaps into the sea
He cuts all the rope
Till the propeller is free

A Messerschmitt, guns blazing
Dives out of the sun
Flying low at Blue Beach Two
It starts a death run

There are holes in our craft
Thank God no one was hit
Our hearts racing wildly
Scared out of our wits

Our crew with the soldiers
There's much we've endured
But we're happy in spirit
Blue Beach Two is secured

A Demon Called Fear

November 1942

What makes a great nation
Allow its allegiance to turn cold

What can make normal people
Suddenly sell their soul

What can force free men
To forfeit their given rights

What can drain the desire
That makes a nation fight

An emotion-controlling demon
Hidden within our souls

When trauma pressure enters
A controlling demon turns us cold

It weakens your will and senses
During anxiety it appears

Completely divesting the weak
A controlling demon called fear

Survivor's Anxiety

November 1942

Trapped below E deck
An escape from Hell

A sinking, torpedoed ship
Yet I lived to tell

Blood and oil on my body
An aching burnt ear

Down the rope ladder
Suddenly a taste of fear

In North African waters
My stomach in knots

The smell of my blood
Will now attract sharks

Before I decide to leap
A landing craft appears

A prayer to thank God
A rescue crew is near

USS Hugh L. Scott (AP-43)

(Courtesy of Naval History and Heritage Command)

There is no information available on the condition of the ship at the time she was attacked. It is known, however, that she was engaged in unloading cargo to the beach at Fedala on 12 November, 1942. At 1732, 12 November, about one minute after the first torpedo hit EDWARD RUTLEDGE, two torpedoes hit SCOTT on the starboard side. There was an appreciable interval (about 10 seconds) between the two explosions. The first torpedo apparently struck the starboard side abreast No. 1 fireroom, and the second probably hit in the engine room. The ship appeared to lift and then immediately listed about 30 degrees to starboard and began to settle aft. All power, lighting & communication went out with the first hit and no auxiliary lighting was available, resulting in complete darkness.

The explosions wrecked all starboard Welin Davits and blew one cross beam up onto the sun deck. It was reported that wooden bulkheads throughout the ship collapsed.

The first torpedo wrecked the galley and mess hall on "D" deck immediately above the firerooms. It also caused the cabin and adjacent rooms under the bridge structure to collapse, apparently from the weight of plastic protection installed above them. Large quantities of fuel flowed out on the water on the starboard side.

When it became apparent that nothing could be done to save the ship, the Commanding Officer ordered the ship abandoned. Boats continued in the vicinity of the ship until about 2030. At that time the ship was still afloat, but she sank some time later during the night.

A Warrior's Mind

November 1942

From everyone's birth
To their final demise
Decisions are made
Some foolish, some wise

A decision that's harder
Than all the rest
The heart-rending choice
Between life and death

Five young seamen
In below the deck quarters
An attack transport
In North African waters

A Nazi torpedo
Rips the ship's side
A loud explosion
And four amphibians die

One lone survivor
In a deadly shock wave
Pinned under lockers
His eyes all a glaze

Flooding sea water
He begins to recoil
His body submerged
In salt water and oil

In despair he calls
Each shipmate by name
Then an echo of silence
His cries are in vain

Bewildered and scared
In dark rising waters
His greatest challenge
Making the hard choices

The compartment now flooded
His mouth to bare steel
He must desperately inhale
Any air he can steal

A high leaking pipe
A loud piercing scream
His inner ear is burned
By escaping hot steam

He must desperately tread water
To stay afloat
The air pockets are small
As is his hope

Now comes that moment
A decision unclear
Fight the inevitable
Or give in to fear

No air's left to breathe
But what is worse
The deadly feeling
That his lungs will soon burst

Amidst his prayers
He still battles his fright
Swimming hard to the surface
For life he will fight

The ship suddenly rolls
Though it seems odd
Was it shifting waters
Or the hand of God

The blast blew a hole
On the room's overhead
On the flooded D deck
Void and darkness ahead

Completely confused
Silent darkness his foe
Bewildered he wonders
Which way will I go

Two steps to his left
Then he suddenly fell
Back down in the hole
In the darkness of Hell

Fighting gripping fatigue
With no sense of time
With one mighty effort
On to D deck he climbs

With the eyes of a blind man
Touch was his guide
He lays his hands on
The cool bulkhead slide

On the top deck, oily and black
His naked soul
Escaped certain death
In the ship's oily hole

The decision he made
Is now quite clear
He finally succeeded
He conquered his fear

Worry, fear, fragile minds
They often stray
Those depressed feelings
They're here to stay

Now he has earned
A warrior's mind
Having faced war and life
One day at a time

Amphibious landing of American troops – November 1942

"Our craft was hit by a low flying German Messerschmitt strafing the beach, the landing crafts and running soldiers. Because we had no craft, the army sergeant said we were to accompany him on a 13 mile walk to Casablanca. There, a navy boat took my crew and I back to the Scott."

Warrior's Dilemma
November 1942

Those endless hours of training
Learning how to control stress
A young amphibian sailor in harm's way
This I feel a final test

A question, a warrior's torment
When in action, what's my fate
Proudly walk the steps of bravery
Or through fear, face disgrace

An inevitable question now the test
My blood pressure starts to drop
My stomach a heavy weight
A constant pounding, a racing heart

Many warriors have often wondered
Exactly what they would do
If suddenly the face of death was standing
Staring at our crew

Amphibian craft, in several rows
Each soldier's face a glare
An enemy shell, a direct hit
A craft and bodies blown in the air

A Messerschmitt, a rain of fire
Four young sailors lie prone
A final dash to the beach
But through fear, legs of stone

A flooded room, four mates dead
One survivor against all odds
Finally overcomes his date with death
With the help of his God

The destructive violence of the action
Has at last finally ceased
This tested warrior defeated doubts and his fear
His alter ego beast

In safer waters, time to reflect
The warrior's outlook now finds
Like a change in metamorphosis
He now takes each day one at a time

USS Hugh L. Scott (AP 43)
American Troop Transport
sunk by German submarine U-130
12 November, 1942

The Torpedo Roadstead
November 1942

Optimistic and bold, Fedhala's roadstead their berth
A prerequisite to defiance, prepared for the worst

At dusk on the eleventh, the situation turned grave
Three ships were torpedoed, two vessels were saved

The Hambleton's listing, Winooski a damaged tank
Joseph Hewes struck amidship, it faulted then sank

The evasive U-173 challenged our frivolous stand
Fired three quick torpedoes, dove deep, then ran

It was the night of the twelfth, eerie feelings are back
A sailor's worst nightmare, a night U Boat attack

The U-130 slipped between mines and the land
Stalking our task force, firing torpedoes as planned

The Scott and the Rutledge, the Tasker Bliss too
Struck by torpedoes, from the U-130s crew

Five men on the Scott, a compartment on E deck
Will soon face a danger that no one expects

The torpedo explodes, crew lockers unhinged
Below them on deck, I'm suddenly pinned

The powerful force, a pressure immense
My chest in a vice, my breathing intense

The rising salt water, compartment a moat
The heavy crew lockers, at last start to float

Room cloaked in darkness, no voice but my own
Four shipmates are dead, I'm now all alone

My mind in a vision, my whole life rushes by
"Oh God," I ask, "What pray is the answer"

Is it deemed that this, is the day I will die
Scott's rivets blown out, I see crafts cruising by

I yell out for help but my plea's a dead cry
The outlook is dismal but to survive I must try

From beyond the bulkhead, I hear frantic cries
Rush to the hatchway to escape or to die

Evacuate Engine Room, a cry from the chief
Up the escape hatch, their efforts were brief

Trapped by high water, both ends of the hatch
Men cried and prayed, this their final act

The fear in their voices, stirred the still air
A feeling of helplessness, total despair

Oh God, my sweet Jesus, help me my Lord
Please hear our pleas, we don't want to die

The compartment is flooded, debris everywhere
I claw at the overhead, fighting for air

Oily water fast rising, the steel overhead bare
My mouth on cold steel, sucking for air

I slip under water, I'm completely submerged
My lungs start to burst, to the surface I surge

The ship rolls abruptly, there's room to breathe
I say a fast prayer, completely relieved

Treading oily water, reaching for what, I don't know
Suddenly, my hands discover a large hole

The blast killed my mates, then upward it soared
It blew a large hole in the Mess Deck floor

With unknown strength, I scale to the Mess Deck
I lie on cold steel, aching, toe to my neck

The passageways in darkness, like a blind man I grope
My mind's in confusion, my heart's in my throat

Up a hatchway I crawl, every moment a prayer
At last, I see light, thank the Lord, I declare

The main deck is vacant, not a human in sight
The ship seems deserted, I continue my flight

Down the Scott's rope ladder I slowly descend
A landing craft nears, my ordeal's at an end

As I lie in the boat, I fought death with no plan
Yet, now I wonder, was I holding God's hand

Troop Transport USS Tasker H. Bliss (AP-42)
Sunk by U-130 during Operation Torch
12 November, 1942

Troop Transport USS Edward Rutledge (AP-52)
Sunk by U-130 during Operation Torch
12 November, 1942

Battleship USS Alabama (BB-60)
During her shakedown period – Casco, Maine, United States
December 1942

A Question Frequently Asked
December 1942

An attack transport in African waters
Below deck quarters, engineers five

A German torpedo, a devastating explosion
Four engineers' dead only one survived

Questions asked, no answer forthcoming
A powerful detonation, an amazing surprise

Five in compartment, steel overhead blasted
Four men are dead, only one still alive

Steel overhead crumbled, men blown apart
Only one human life defeated the odds

A life indestructible or a gift from God
The answer simple, understanding is hard

Four

1943

John E. O'Hara, Gun Captain
40 MM Antiaircraft Quad 8
USS Alabama Battleship
(Courtesy of John E. O'Hara)

Working on one of USS Alabama's boilers
January 1943

Arctic Action

January 1943

In the early months of Forty-three
During the Second World War
Operations of united forces
Fought together as a single corp

This particular story of this war operation
Has seldom been told
Of a joint war action that was fought
In weather so cold

The American and the British
Combined naval task forces
Cruised the cold Arctic waters
To increase the Nazi's losses

Two torpedoed amphibians
Of the North African invasion
Turned down the shore duty
For Alabama's accommodations

Gordon "Flash" Raynor and I had served
On the ill-fated USS Scott
Now the battleship USS Alabama
Was our choice and our lot

The Alabama's first port of call
Maine's frozen Casco Bay
One night of granted liberty pass
And we were on our way

We dropped anchor in Argentina Bay
Weather foggy and cold
It's a land that's barren of trees
So dreary, weary and old

Our ship casts off at the break of dawn
Sailing north and east
Our ship fights rough weather
The rolling waves increase

As solid walls of cold sea water
Crashed over our port side
"Stay clear of the main deck"
Was the ship boatswain's cry

The boatswain piped and yelled
"If you're washed over the side
The water temperature's so cold
There's no way you can survive"

Through the mist and rain we sailed
Through the Pentland Firth
Then we sailed north to Scapa Flow
Anchored at our assigned berth

The crew leaned over the USS Alabama's side
The scene a happy treat
We finally were viewing the ships
Of the British Home Fleet

In cold, foul blowing weather
Our battle stations were manned
Then slipping our mooring
The task force set sail for Iceland

The Country of Iceland, like Orkney
Is land that's timeless
As one shipmate yelled out
"This is a land that is timeless"

The PA blasted, "All hands turn to
We're loading food and stock"
The crew patiently waited for
Iceland's skies to get dark

We kept hauling food and other supplies
Thought we'd never be done
We suddenly realized that we were
In the Land of the Midnight Sun

We sail, this time to the west
North through the Denmark Straits
We cross over the Arctic Circle
Blue noses is what we create

Alabama sails the Southwest Passage
Fjord cliffs reach high
The air is very cold, it's frigid now
And mist conceal the sky

The next morning, now at anchor
Thick ice hangs from our guns
Using shovels, picks, and brooms
We're all wishing for the sun

We sailed back into Arctic waters
A bright reddishness soon arose
The crew now must wear a face mask
To cover our frozen nose

Sailing to our rallying point
Near Spit Bergen's Eastern Coast
We're shadowing the merchant convoy
Like a silent, frozen ghost

The German's pocket battleship, the Tirpitz
With cruisers in their rank
Should soon attack the convoy
Shelling merchant ships till they sank

But the Tirpitz never sailed
And the Luftwaffe is now on our back
We manned our anti-aircraft guns
In a thirteen hour attack

Our Arctic covert operation
As part of a combined allied task force
Now at an end
The United States Fleet Commanders orders us home

We are cold, we are tired, we are exhausted
Every sailor hits the sack
A long sail across the rough
Atlantic Ocean to the Panama Zone

Battleship USS Alabama (BB-60)

Off Norfolk Naval Shipyard, Virginia, United States
returning from the Arctic
20 August, 1943

The Goony Birds

August 1943

Port and Starboard catapults
On Bama's aft main deck
Hold two twin Vought Kingfishers
They're ready to eject

The Kingfishers are no Hell Cats
The crew passed the word
"Those slow flying planes
They're called our Goony Birds"

Dawn's first light was breaking
A salty mist was everywhere
The catapult crew was working
To launch Kingfishers in the air

The pilot revs the Goony Bird's engine
And it makes a mighty roar
Blue flames from twin exhausts snort wildly
Just like wild boar

There's a sudden loud explosion
The pilot's head is thrown back
The plane goes from zero to sixty knots
70 feet down the track

The Goony Bird drops slightly
Then soars into the blue
It's heading for a battle mission
Keeping a course that is true

To spot our ship's bombardments
Over enemy islands they fly
Spotting submarines and rescue pilots
They were Alabama's eyes

The Alabama's high speed turns
Create a smooth ocean wake
Wild ocean waves dancing high
Become calm for landing's sake

Condition of the sea state
Made recovery, condition red
Until the sea plane's main pontoon
Is latched onto the sea sled

The Kingfisher's engine is shut off
The radio mask turned down
Bridle connected to hoist hook
Then the Goony Bird's catapult bound

Ancient Orders
September 1943

"Tradition, tradition," sang Topol
In *Fiddler on the Roof*
The US Navy, draped in tradition
A prelude to the truth

The Sea Gods of the frozen North
In an ancient writ
Grant special honors to seamen
With courage and true grit

We crossed the great Arctic Circle
Where even life is frozen
We all became life members
Of Ancient Order of Blue Noses

The beautiful Pacific on September one
Nineteen-forty-three
The Royal Court of Davy Jones
With an air of enormity

King Neptune sends a message
To a commander of our ship
Apprised that lowly pollywogs
Have joined him on this trip

The King graciously consented
To let the Alabama proceed
But all pollywogs and landlubbers
An innovation they must heed

Shell Backs in good standing
Filled sewn canvas tubes with water
To initiate scared pollywogs
Into Neptune's Ancient Order

Shell Backs oiled our chests
And our hair they hacked
With swinging paddles
Declared us "Shell Backs"

All landlubbers and pollywogs
Have the respect they seek
But shillelaghs well aimed
We didn't sit for a week

September eleventh, 1943
In Asian waters we sail on
Across the 180th meridian
To become Golden Dragons

In just four short months
In fateful Forty-three
Golden Dragon, Blue Nose, Shell Backs
We have three ancient degrees

The Shell Backs

September 1943

The Alabama sails on a sea of mirrors
While Panama just fades away
Crossing over Equator's waters
Where Neptune's daughters love to play

Sleeping soundly in their quarters
Dreaming, snorting, grunts and groans
The PA blasts a startling message
"We've just piped aboard Davy Jones

Attention all you salty seasoned sailors
Of the Alabama's loyal crew
Round up every green pollywog
Prepare them for ole King Neptune's stew"

His Royal Majesty, with indignation
"Shell Backs now man your stations
Gather up those lowly pawns
Our ancient rites will change their forms"

In weird costumes they sang off-tune
From break of day through 'til noon
Lone rods with wire, an electric shock
If singing stops, we all get shocked

Neptune's sewn canvas tables on the aft deck
Initiate each slimy green suspect
With skill, wash away each pollywog
Then dress them in shell back togs

With hair cut short and our oily, hairy chests
The water dunking was a melee
Our manly pride was badly bruised
By shell back's paddles and shillelaghs

Those once presumptuous pollywogs
Now unmasked by Neptune's ancient facts
Will proudly stroll Alabama's decks
Restricted to Neptune's loyal shell backs

Ahoy, all ye lowly green pollywogs
And you landlubbers on this steel craft
Beware of all us shell backs
Because we are part of King Neptune's staff

The Shooter
November 1943

A liberty on a Pacific atoll
Meant lots of sand but no dames
A blanket spread full length
Shooters in line for a crap game

There was real excitement
When an experienced shooter threw
The dice well-shaken, tossed
They roll over to five and two

The stakes keep growing
And lots of greenbacks change hands
Watching every style and motion
And how rolling dice will land

The winning sailor kept shooting
Lots of money changed hands
Watching each shooter's movement
And how the dice will land

One lanky sailor kept shooting
He kept making pass after pass
The ante kept growing
Everyone wonders how long this can last

The sailor then drops to one knee
And on those dice he would blow
He makes a pass, number seven
And his winnings continue to grow

"I think he's using passers"
Doubting the shooter's winning streak
Then the lanky, lucky shooter
Very quickly jumped to his feet

"Hey man, toss me those bones
The ones you claim you trained"
The startled shooter stared
Then said, "Hey man, you're insane"

The shooter's dice hands lifted high
He makes a mighty toss
The square bones land on atoll sand
The dice, I fear, are lost

There are about a hundred men on this beach
Walking all around
No one claims they've seen the dice
When they actually hit the ground

But the dice-shooting players all scramble
Begin to sift the sand
But their sifting effort all in vain
As the lanky sailor is on the lam

The players shift from sifting sand
Find the sailor with a special touch
A sailor in white
Is impossible to find

We're back at sea, sailing smoothly
The gambling bug has survived
A blanket spread near the smokestacks
A card game comes to life

The green back kitty, so I was told
Is starting to grow rather high
The ship suddenly turns to starboard
In the wind the kitty rides

Laying aft on the fantail,
Suddenly there are greenbacks floating by
A division, detail-working crew
Was grabbing dollars from the sky

SBD Dauntless Dive Bomber
On the flight deck of the Enterprise

Leadership
December 1943

Some experts claim good leaders are born
Other scholars say this assumption is wrong
Some experts claim that anyone can lead
If they study hard and are well trained
This group I say is not a rare breed
A leader is needed from out of the thorn
They all stand in line, the line is not long
Only desire and the will to serve
Regardless of training or being born
Will finally design the right leader
So both experts are wrong

Five

1944

USS Intrepid
On her way to launch strikes against Truk Atoll
with SBD Dauntless and TBF Avenger aircraft
on her deck 26 January, 1944

Securing the Marshalls
January 1944

The Gilbert Islands have fallen
Nauru's helpless rock
The taking of the Marshalls
Navy Code, Flintlock

Japanese Admiral Koga
Playing it by the book
Breaking up the landings
His assault force at Truk

Operation Flintlock
Japanese were well aware
Spruance's fast task force
Can strike from anywhere

Admiral Koga played a hunch
Perused the Island's map
"Spruance will invade the
Islands of Wotje and Maloelap"

Admiral Nimitz and his staff
Developed a surprise strategy
Attack Marshall's strongest island
Kwajalein's the key

Spruance set our course
Sail west past Namu Atoll
Battleships in formation
Kwajalein bombing their goal

Seven new fast battlewagons
Then veered off one by one
"Commence firing broadside"
Saturation had begun

A pre-invasion bombardment
By the fleet's juggernauts
Gave the Island of Tarawa
A Spruance's haircut

Intermittent rain squalls
Concealed from air attack
An air attack fills the sky
With rapid naval flak

The radar's tracking bogies
Flying high from the North
Eighteen escort fighters and Betty's
On a bombing course

The crew goes into action
Our squad becomes alive
Firing at Zekes and Zeros
As they peel into a dive

Each projectile in cadence
Their line of trajectory high
Each in systematic rhythm
Tracers illuminate the sky

Our bodies tired and weary
At battle station we'll stay
On this unknown journey
As we sail into harm's way

The anticipation and confusion
Of Japan's high command
The crescendo of our victories
Stars and Stripes on Nippon land

The neutralization of the Marshalls
By Task Force fifty-eight
The pulverization of the islands
Put our fleet at Japan's gate

The Month of March

March is the month that appeals to me
Restoring nature's springtime colors

And painting green God's forest trees
As strong cold winter winds finally

Regenerate to spring nature's shift
A special change, March's enduring gift

The month divided between fish and ram
Cold winds ended as a new spring began

On sturdy tree limbs, redbreast robin sing
Awakening all life, throughout God's land

Task Force 58 of the
US Navy 5th Fleet at anchor
Majuro Atoll, Marshall Islands
April 1944

Analyzing Anger
May 1944

A predator within your deep emotion
A dormant demon quietly hides
Waiting for one violent moment
Your anger demon now your guide

Mortal erotic metamorphosis
Common sense eclipsed, then washed away
Your demon anger consumed in evil glory
Self control has gone astray

A spoken word, a mistaken gesture
A disappointment, an emotional event
Now quickly rising consuming anger
A demon's message has been sent

The growing anger becoming toxic
Quickly festering to uncontrollable hate
An act of passion through physical exertion
Controls your anguish, your fate

Your mind, your soul, your very being
Has suffered a terrible crushing blow
Your aching heart feels sad and heavy
But after pain continually grows

A lamp of goodness now diminished
Your curse the weakness of your soul
Experiencing the loss of your integrity
You pray for the soul that anger stole

The Death of A Hero
May 1944

Our Task Force 58 sailed passed the Admiralty Islands as we completed the bombardment of Weewak and Hollandia in New Guinea. This task force has been at sea for the past four months, attacking Japanese strongholds in the Pacific. Suddenly, a nice surprise, mail call. Hell, we haven't had mail call since December 1943, months ago. I received a tied bundle of letters. I had just finished reading four of them when I opened a letter from my father. I quickly read the first page, stopped and reread it again. My stomach felt clogged, my throat went dry and I felt a strange pressure around my heart.

Those six words in my father's letter completely clouded my thoughts, "Your cousin Sunny Lomas was killed." The letter continued, "His PBY exploded when he tried to land." I left the main deck and headed aft to the fantail as I was afraid I might cry and did not want to break down in front of the crew. I opened my notebook, as I did whenever I felt wound up and wrote a poem about my thoughts. (See facing page.)

William Warren Lomas, our Sunny, was the oldest boy in the family. He was three years my senior and had graduated from Northeastern University in the later part of the 1930s. America had not yet entered the war in 1938. He went to Canada and joined the Canadian Air Force and was assigned to Britain's Royal Air Force (RAF). He flew missions in the flak-filled skies over Germany for five years until he transferred to the US Navy Air Force in 1943 as a Lt. Commander. He was flying a PBY on a submarine reconnaissance off the coast of Curacao in the Caribbean Sea. According to the information the family received on the death of William Lomas, Sunny was on a submarine reconnaissance and a depth charge or a canister was jammed and landing the plane was going to be a problem. Sunny had his crew parachute to safety, but instead of abandoning the plane, he tried to land the PBY and it exploded, killing him instantly.

Lt. Commander William Warren Lomas, after flying bombing missions over Germany from 1939 until 1943, was transferred to the US Navy in 1943. We will never know why Sunny tried to land the PBY after bailing the crew out, knowing so well the dangers he faced.

Forever Spirit
May 1944

A letter from home:

*My cousin, Sunny Lomas was killed in the Atlantic.
How can I understand this family loss?*

The body's just an outer shell
An earthly form to fit God's need
The spirit, soul so carefully placed
Is now a gift from God's holy seed

When you die, do you really die?
Although the body's laid to rest
Your soul and spirit are gifts from God
Believing Sunny's dead, just too hard

Within the wind and God's soaring birds
Departed spirits now reside
Sending a message of their love
These spirits are now our Heavenly guides

US Navy PB4Y-2 Privateer on patrol – similar to Sunny's

The Thrill of Nature
June 1944

There's nothing as invigorating as watching angry rolling waves
Their frothy teeth so very white, crashing on rocks in a misty maze

A sight so stirringly intriguing, sunset mixtures of spectrum lights
Dashes of orange, bright yellow, mixtures of shades an awesome sight

The sun supplies the spectrum as clouds peek-a-boo with the sprays
The ocean mirrors streaks of light, ending another beautiful day

Looking Into the Face of Death
June 1944

Task Force 38 entered the waters
Off Engano Bay at dusk
The final showdown between
Two rival battle fleets

Admiral "Bull" Halsey and
Elusive Imperial Admiral Ozawa
Knew that on this day one fleet
Would go down in defeat

The angry Pacific waters east to Luzon
Were not a friendly sight
A constant stream of air attacks
Ozawa's ready for a fight

Suddenly, from Formosa
A Kamikaze in the overhead clouds
Disappeared for a moment
Then turned its nose into a dive

Every anti-aircraft gun was pointed
Up at the twilight sky
The suicide fighter was determined
That no one would survive

Our five inch thirty eights
And 40 mm guns sprayed the sky
The 5" 38s and 40mm quads
Shells tried to keep us alive

The Alabama then made a high speed
Sharp starboard turn
The Kamikaze fighter crashed
Off port side in the gray sea

Each gun crew in silence
Stared and watched the Zero burn
Gazing in disbelief, our inner fears
At last survived the melee

Within their inner thoughts
Gunners know they passed the test
This was the eventful day
Our crew stared into the face of death

General Paul Muella welcoming Admiral William Halsey (right)
to Angaur, Palau Islands, November 1944

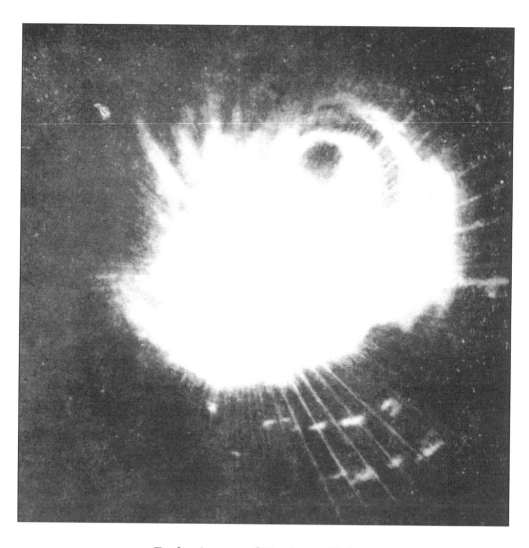

Radar image of Typhoon Cobra
captured by radar system of a US Navy ship
18 December, 1944

Tempest Called Cobra
December 1944

Armor-piercing shells
From our sixteen inch guns
Tear up Guam's stronghold
Japanese on the run

The battle fleet of Ozawa
Spotted eastward by scouts
Our Task Force is ready
Night encounter no doubt

Admiral "Bull" Halsey and Ozawa
Is a feud that burns bright
But Admiral Ozawa
Chooses flight o'er sea fight

The Marinas now behind us
And new targets to seek
On to the Philippine Islands
And Admiral Kurita's fleet

It's become a daily occurrence
To sail into harm's way
We are needed at Leyte Gulf
Admiral Kurita is our pray

First we must have a rendezvous
With the fleet's oilers
To fill the ship's oil tanks
Which feed the ship's boilers

The Pacific's getting choppy
The winds growing strong
The fuel area getting darker
There's threat of a storm

The calmness of this ocean
Turns dark and robust
The sea shows its anger
With the waves' powerful thrust

Refueling becomes difficult
As the ships bob and roll
Every slippery fuel hose
Has become too hard to control

The tropical disturbance
Has turned hazardous by noon
And the storm's been updated
Into a full blown typhoon

A tempest called Cobra
Roars counter-clock winds
Spits thunder and lightning
Crawls, coils then springs

The Third Fleet rolls sharply
Rolls to seventy degrees
As cyclonic wind velocity
Feeds a violent, angry sea

Smaller ships slip into an abyss
Between violent waves
Into escape-proof "Irons"
The ship's condition now grave

The bow of the USS Alabama
Rises out of the water
Dives deep under high waters
That gives no quarters

The next morning
Still lost in a strange violent force
High winds have increased
And shifted to the north

Many carrier planes
Are washed over the carrier's side
Crushed decks, a lost hull
And many crewmen died

The Epilogue of the Cobra
A storm with dark skies
After violent destruction
It kills, then it dies

Nature's Power
1944

Man's military might and his huge arsenals
With powerful weapons of mass destruction

Compared to the power within nature's force
Man's deadly weapons are a minor production

The Shawnee Indians often tell a legend
About why Mother Earth suddenly shakes

The great Sky Spirit would stamp his feet
And create a major earthquake

Mother Nature has the destructive strength
To maliciously create a mega thrust

That's equal to one million atomic bombs
Causing powerful shifts in the earth's crust

Trembling, a shudder, and here comes another
The awesome power of the sea's giant waves

That attack, the beaches with reckless force
And for those in its path make a watery grave

Nature's typhoons, hurricanes and tornadoes
Reap mass destruction both on land and sea

Leaving in its wide, arrogant, destructive wake
A lasting aftermath of sorrow and dead debris

TBF Avenger Aircraft
With its gear, flaps, and hook down

The Invasion Never Made
July 1944

A slightly-built man of power
On a sandy beach in France
Stood glaring across the channel
His mind lost in a trance

He covets the shores of England
As he stands from dawn to dusk
"We must invade the British Isles"
His desire turned to lust

Weeks after France surrendered
The British hold their stance
"If they don't surrender
My troops will invade their land"

The Fuhrer sent a proposal
To the British High Command
"Your situation is hopeless
You must accept our demands"

Britain rejects the proposal
To make England a German base
Hitler orders his Luftwaffe
To lay the British Isles to waste

Hitler's Operation Sea Lion
By his navy's landing corps
Will overrun Kent and Sussex
As they knock on England's door

But the navy's grand admiral
Half-heartedly endorsed the plan
While the air defense of England
Was nothing short of grand

The target date for Sea Lion
As Goring's Luftwaffe tried
Now prolonged to a later date
As the RAF controls the sky

Delayed from July until August
And finally to next spring
The Eastern Front was boiling
And Sea Lion lost its sting

Hitler's Operation Sea Lion
Over the months began to fade
The fighting heart of England
Stopped the invasion never made

Isle of Sadness
September 1944

The three militarized islands
In the Mariana chain
Guam, Saipan, and Titia
But Saipan was our aim

The ready-made air base
Those long landing lanes
Made the choice of Saipan
Ideal for larger planes

Saito, Island Commander
Feared amphibious forces
Would inflict upon his army
Serious major losses

Assembling all his soldiers
Saito put them all at rest
"Whether we attack or stay
For us there is only death"

Mustering all their courage
Made several futile stands
The amphibians then drove them
Far back into the land

Saito told Saipan village natives
Although he told a lie
"Those Evil American Devils
Will beat you till you die"

Villagers afraid, disillusioned
Obeyed Saito's demands
Climbed up to Morubi Bluff
And awaited his command

They utilized the moment
To exalt their ancient rites
Their deity had taught them
In death there is life

Villagers' minds in disarray
And paranoid about their foe
Jumped off the craggy cliffs
To the rocks and surf below

The Japanese General stared
In anguish at 8,000 lying dead
He committed Hari Kari
His adjutant shot a bullet in his head

John remembers a close encounter with the hereafter that happened in the waters off Formosa. "That was a day I will never forget. The sky way darkened with storm clouds. The ocean was angry and lashing out like a mad dog. Japanese planes were hedge hopping low to the sea. This forced our ships to fire low with the possibility of hitting one of our own. Unfortunately that is exactly what happened. Suddenly a warning came through my head phones; a Kamikaze was directly over our ship. Our guns were firing straight up towards the Heavens. 'It's diving at us!' Those were the words of desperation that filled my ears. 'Keep firing, keep firing' I yelled. The plane started to dive. The Alabama made a hard turn to starboard and the Kamikaze crashed and exploded in the ocean off our port side. My heart was pounding from fear, then relief. How did that plane miss us? How did we survive that battle without losing a man? We must have been blessed."

Kamikaze Attack
Octoberber 1944

The Japanese Air Force
In a "Turkey Shoot" bout
Suffered a devastating defeat
Was largely wiped out

A new Japanese weapon
Enter Sho-Gun One
With suicide pilots
Kamikazes were born

The word "Kami" means "holy"
And "Kaze" the wind
These young suicide pilots
Now called holy winds

A sea battle off Cape Engano
A lone Kamikaze flies
Above the battleship Alabama
Very high in the sky

The Kamikaze plane dips its nose
Then starts to dive
The Kamikaze's holy mission
To eliminate our lives

All the ship's guns are firing
Straight into the air
Firing very rapidly
With all they can bear

"The Kamikaze is diving"
Gun crew's impulsive cries
"It's going to crash into us
We're all going to die"

The gun captain yells
At the top of his lungs
"Keep firing, keep firing
And keep firing those guns"

The Alabama turns sharply
To starboard, a degree
The Kamikaze to portside
Explodes in the sea

The crew looks at each other
Disbelief on their face
But no one admitted
Our heart, that day raced

Tokyo Rose, the next day
So serious and frank
Reported on radio
"The USS Alabama has sank"

Well, Miss Tokyo Rose
I have good news for you
The battleship Alabama
Still sails as well as its crew

THE BATTLE OFF
CAPE ENGANO
OCTOBER 24, 1944

Battleship USS Alabama (BB-60)

The battle off Cape Engano
24 October, 1944
(Courtesy of John E. O'Hara)

A Deadly Foe

October 1944

A spider web sky of misty gray clouds
A destructive force, a Kamikaze dives
Chilling wet sea winds, an October quest
The Alabama within his target sight

Off Cape Engano, the Philippine sea
A great naval battle now being fought
40 mm shells paint a polka dot sky
The day I saw the face of death

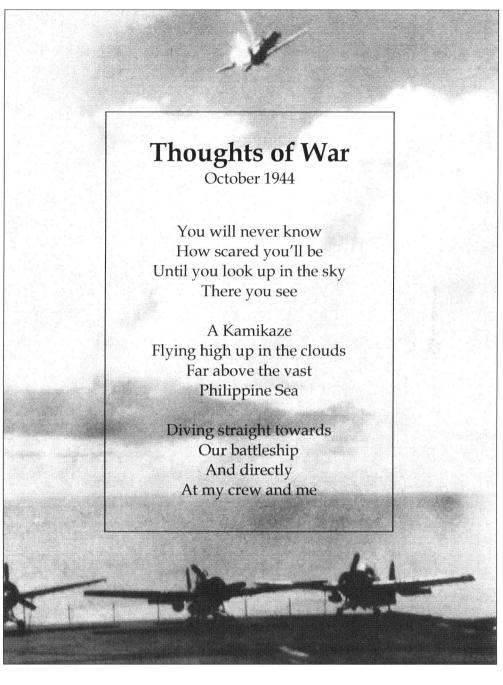

Thoughts of War
October 1944

You will never know
How scared you'll be
Until you look up in the sky
There you see

A Kamikaze
Flying high up in the clouds
Far above the vast
Philippine Sea

Diving straight towards
Our battleship
And directly
At my crew and me

Flaming Kamikaze special attack plane
falling astern of Petrof Bay
Philippine Islands
26 October, 1944

USS Copahee

Passing under the Golden Gate Bridge
San Francisco Bay, California, United States
15 July, 1944

Seaward Bound

November 1944

Liberty days have ended, Alabama's underway
Frisco now is fading, on the horizon on the bay

Sea routine takes over under orders of the day
Scrubbing decks, cleaning guns, all is done the Navy way

The PA suddenly crackles a message we all hate
"Lineup-dress inspection" Sailing under Golden Gate

There are a thousand white caps
Lined up row on row
We are ready for inspection
And rigid head to toe

Inspections nearly over
Command "Stand at ease"
A slight taste of salt
In a warm summer breeze

The Pacific, so peaceful
Like an ocean made of glass
Words from salty veterans
"This weather never lasts"

Navy crew's favorite habit
A cup of steaming Joe
That's what mates call coffee
As every seaman knows

Meantime near the smokestacks
High rollers risk their pay
Shaking small square dotted bones
Roll them, let them lay

"I think I see a tornado"
Some new recruit shouts
A petty officer corrects him
"That's just a water spout"

Our ship in fleet formation steams towards harm's way
Proven battle veterans face death, day by day by day

Bogies have been spotted, "All hands man your guns"
They're diving at our ship, the battle has begun

Our forty millimeter rounds form a true trajectory
In synchronizing rhythm bogies crash into the sea

The Great Mariana Turkey Shoot
November 1944

Admiral Ozawa's carrier fleet
With Imperial pilots well-trained
Launched an air power strike
With 450 Japanese carrier planes

"Fighter pilots now man your planes"
The ship's PA blasts
Pilots sprint across the decks
With chart board and oxygen masks

Mitcher's fleet and ten large carriers
Turn quickly into the wind
A record time in launching
With their one thought, to win

The Fifth Fleet's Hell Cats'
Fast fighters soon flooded the air lanes
Their official standard orders
To engage when the enemy's in range

To increase their greater range
Japan built their fighter planes lighter
Leaving out the protecting armor plating
That shields their pilot fighters

The enemy was sighted on the nineteenth
Dueled continuously all day
This great naval air battle
Blew Admiral Ozawa's air force away

What started as a naval fighter duel
Finished as a turkey shoot slaughter
Marc Mitscher's Hell Cat fighters
Gave the Japanese planes no quarter

The result of our naval fighters' skills
For Admiral Ozawa it was plain
Of his four hundred thirty vast naval air power
Only thirty five planes remain

Tired, weary American pilots
Flying above a darkened watery waste
Broke the code of radio silence
"I need a course to find the base"

The American pilots were exhausted
Fuel tanks were dangerously low
Some returning planes' engines cough
Cut out, then down they go

A disaster waiting to happen
The complete darkness now their fright
Then Marc Mitscher gave the unexpected order
"Turn on the lights"

Disregarding enemy dangers
Ship's searchlights lit up the sky
The fleets' destroyers fired star shells
That guided our planes flying high

Admiral Mitscher's act of compassion
A bold, courageous life-saving feat
Led our lost fighter planes
To land safely on an illuminated fleet

"The Great Turkey Shoot"
The battle that finally sealed the Japanese fate
Now recorded in our history
As the greatest naval air battle to date

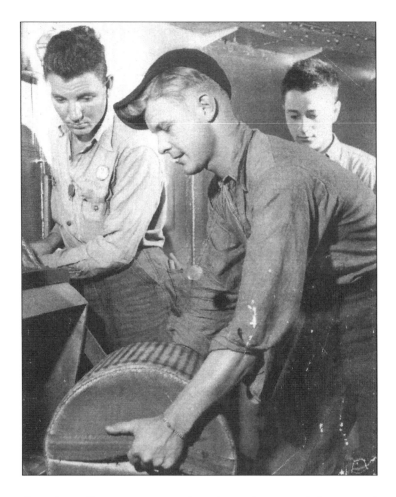

Sailors handling gun powder aboard USS Alabama, 1944

John remembers: "An unforgettable event that still lingers in my mind happened aboard the USS Alabama, in the Pacific, during a long night air attack off the Marshall Islands. I was the gun captain on Quad 8, a 40mm gun site, when my ammo passers told me there was a fire in the ammo compartment. I remember looking at the compartment and seeing men running out of the hatchway. I tore off my head set and helmet then ran into the compartment, throwing the ammo cans away from the fire, stamping out the fire and smoldering rags and string. I returned to my post and realized that my crew was staring at me. Then reality hit me. I was alone in that fire, I could have been blown up at any second. I did not even think of that possibility, only saving the ammo. I still wonder why the ammo did not explode."

A Mistress Called the Sea

December 1944

Sat for hours as a young boy
Watching waves so loose and free

Massaging each loose beach sand
With cool, gentle, watery hands

There are times the waves just disappear
The sea then becomes smooth as glass

Then each wave will break and race
From the dark night till the dawn

High waves will attack the rocky shores
Their wet tongues snap like whips

Then quickly retreat into oncoming waves
Preparing for another repeated trip

A Northeaster is a very angry wind
Churns up the waters that it reaches

Tosses the ships around like little toys
Spits thick gray foam on sandy beaches

A Virus Called Dependency
1944

A Depression virus called dependency
Invaded America's lower class society

To protect a suffering, retreating existence
Has now become that class's top priority

Those past dreams of rising above one's caste
No longer nurtured the young people's mind

Depression years and high unemployment
Forced many poor people to turn to crime

The mentality of long dark Depression years
When all poor classes were blended into one

The traditional trademarks of the family father
Were always passed down to each of his sons

Depression years, a dark emotional burden of need
People prayed for Devine intervention

To be their holy guide and Heavenly sentinel
To ease the suffering and release life's tensions

USS Petrof Bay
On her shakedown cruise
18 March, 1944

Growing Fears
1944

The quiet silence of the darkness
My imagination's deadly foe

As those thoughts of evil demons
In my dreams they seem to grow

As a child my Gnomes were little
They seem to grow the more I age

In my dreams Gnomes grow larger
Becomes my fear an awaking rage

A Christmas Reality
December 1944

The streets are dressed for Christmas
Icicle tinsels float in the winter breeze

Christmas music fills the air waves
Bulbs white and colored light up the trees

Children laugh and roll in the snow
All dressed warmly from winter's cold

Presents packed under Christmas trees
For everyone, both young and old

People deep in Yule time blessings
Exchanging greetings from their soul

But under bridges and city alleys
Our nation's homeless fight the cold

Six

1945

WASP Pilot Elizabeth L. Gardner
At the window of her B-26 Marauder bomber
Harlingen Army Air Field
Texas, United States, circa 1942-1945

Seattle Liberty

January 1945

The Liberty bell is ringing
Eager sailors on the run
Invading Seattle's nightlife
The ship's shore leave has begun

Up those very steep hills of Seattle
The hallmark of its fame
Overhead the clouds are rolling
The dark ones filled with rain

Noisy bars and well-lit night clubs
Attract sailors from the fleet
Those sea-logged lonely sailors
Eager for a dame to meet

A shiny, crowed wooden bar
Perhaps Texan in its style
Inundated with love-starved sailors
The temperament is mild

The peaceful mood is broken
As a sailor's glass held high
"The South Dakota is the greatest"
Blood pressures start to rise

Voices from the crowed bar
"That statement, man, is really sick
The battlewagon you're referring to
We call the 'Shitty Dick'."

The scene, a full blown melee
As fists and bottles fly
A hollow thud, a sudden pain
Now a blackening of my eye

Flying jugs and other objects
Like missiles fired in the air
A sailor lying on the deck
Both his eyes locked in a stare

Loud whistles of the shore patrol
We rush to EXIT signs
No use wasting shore leave
In a boring brig doing time

Out in the rain I said to "Flash"
"You hit me in the eye
When you took a wild swing
At the South Dakota guy"

Puzzled, "Flash" glanced at me
"In the mist of the fight
A sea of white in my sight
All bar room sailors look alike"

The Secrets of the Samurai
January 1945

The secret of the Samurai
They faced death without fear
Ruled the great Japanese Empire
For many an ancient year

Their gift of Shinto concentration
To block out thoughts of death
Their minds immune to pain
Those earthly fears laid to rest

The Samurai Warriors endowed
With bravery, honor, discipline
Their lineage, personal honor, loyalty
And suicides are not a sin

The code of the Samurai Warrior
Faces death before dishonor
Escapes the situation
Accepting the pain the suicide act bore

Created through necessity
In a new operation called Sho-Gun One
Young Japanese pilots that were
Devoted to the Rising Sun

The newly-formed Kamikaze pilot
Devoted to the Rising Sun
His plane replaced a ceremonial sword
As a new era had begun

The Doggerbank
March 1945

The elusive queen of hide and seek
Under ocean skies in fog so deep
The blockade runner of World War Two
Outfitted with a hand-picked crew

World War One now eight years past
A merchant ship so sleek, so fast
By skilled hands this ship was made
In the British Isles her keel was laid

The Indian Ocean in Nineteen-forty-two
The Speybank came under Atlantis gun
The British freighter was forced to yield
To the famous German raider's zeal

The British believed their Speybank sank
The Germans renamed her Doggerbank
Her speed, her size, her fate now cast
Mine-laying operations her new task

Mine-laying crews with nerves of steel
Possess the quickness of a slippery eel
She lays mines in the convoy's path
Dodging patrol boats, then retreating fast

And poses a difficult profile to single out
But Doggerbank's future is now in doubt
Mine-laying operations has now ceased
For blockade-running in the Far East

Her perilous journey to Asia's door
From Yokohama, Saigon and Singapore
Carrying was commodities by the ton
Bolstering Germany's was production

Steaming hard towards the Southern Cross
Then back to Germany, her priority course
But then a Liberator spotted her wake
On the Indian Ocean her safety at stake

She spreads a Union Jack on her forecastle
Hoping to keep a bad situation in check
Using cunning deception, the pretender's tool
Signaling, "SS Inverbank out of Liverpool"

This blockade runner, the sea dog of the deep
Slips past the Allies through dense fog she creeps
There is danger lurking with every sound
Through enemy waters she holds her ground

This crafty pretender in March Forty-five
Off the shores of the Azores steaming free
An Allied merchant ship her pretense
The crew's anticipation now grows intense

Radio silence now must be maintained
This idyllic ghost runner has never waned
The captain's strict orders read like this
"Stay south of the Equator until the Fifth"

Favorable winds plus the very calm seas
Ahead of schedule maintain normal speed
The final leg home seems so very near
A U-boat's Captain is totally confused

The Doggerbank quickly flashed a coded signal
The block runner's signalman's most urgent task
Then very quickly a large German ensign
Was ordered, "Hoist up the ship's mainmast"

In the distance a suspicious German U-boat
But their response was never flashed
The Doggerbank waited minute after minute
And each minute very tediously passed

Three long agonizing hours later
The German U-boat again appeared
They finally flashed their recognition
Then just as quickly disappeared

The U-boat of the Tummer Group
Silently stalking, it lay in wait
The amazing and elusive block runner
Slipped boldly by the U-boat in her wake

But lady luck soon leaves the Queen
Their thoughts of home now a dream
An anxious U-boat their quota to fill
Stalked the freighter, moved in for the kill

The poor unsuspecting Doggerbank
Still steaming forward in a straight line
A nervous, anxious Doggerbank crew
Pointed frantically at their German Ensign

Three fired torpedoes rip through the tide
Into the unsuspecting freighter's exposed side
A loud explosion but no place to hide
As the ship's crew scrambled, still many died

A fate the freighter's crew always dreads
Their Doggerbank, their Queen is dead
The ocean floor is where she will rest
But what the Queen did, she did the best

British Freighter Speybank

The German commerce raider Atlantis,
disguised as the Norwegian freighter Tamesis
fired upon, stopped and captured the British Freighter.
31 January, 1941

The Speybank was converted into the auxiliary mine-layer.
They renamed it, Schiff 53/Doggerbank.

The Lone Survivor

March 1945

The once maneuverable Doggerbank
A volatile cargo, exploding tanks
A crippled hulk, a raging fire
A horrible stench of burning tires

Pillars of black oil burned
Smoke rose in curls then drifted so high
Mixing with the feathered clouds
Darkening the clear Atlantic skies

Blown overboard by three large blasts
For one in three, death came fast
Debris and oil, a flaming sea
Confused, dazed men try swimming free

The tide of fortune now reversed
In its stead a wartime curse
The elusive Queen now has died
The consequence of a foolish pride

A young boatswain at life still claws
Broken body and hands burned raw
Shockingly desperate is how he felt
Too dazed, too tired to even yell for help

Men were crazed with open wounds
Coughing, crying from acid fumes
Some cried out from excruciating pain
Other survivors finally went insane

One small dingy, their act of hope
Tied several oars and rigged a sailboat
Drifting westward and no water to spare
Their future outlook an air of despair

Boar's captain, a shrewd, respected man
Considers conditions, has a mercy plan
Points his gun at each crewmen's head
Then one by one shoots them dead

His face like stone with no sign of fear
Yet down his cheek rolled one tear
Looked at the stoker, he said goodbye
A shot to his head, his time to die

The dinghies were spotted drifting west
Sixteen hundred miles, just a guess
The wind-tattered sailboat passed the test
But only one unconscious survivor left

Heavy Cruiser USS Indianapolis

Torpedoed by Japanese submarine I-58
the ship capsized and sank in less than 15 minutes.
316 men of the 1199 crew were rescued.
30 July, 1945

The Indianapolis had already completed its major mission and was returning from Tinian Island after having delivered key components of the atomic bomb that would be dropped at Hiroshima a week later.

The Ship's Bulletin
August 1945

The ship's company in a straight line
Watches a solemn burial at sea
Makes each sea warrior now realize
Just how short life can be

Uncertain feelings deep in our hearts
A mind that never rests
A transformation, a hard compassion
Blocking out the face of death

Thoughts of shipmates now deceased
Emotionally strain our memories
As an invisible shell engulfs our pride
To help to conceal our vulnerability

A calm Pacific Ocean in August
Then a sudden cold salt water spray
Then a quick brisk cold water shower
To accelerate our busy day

The ship's daily bulletin released
A story with a tragic force
The heavy cruiser USS Indianapolis
Blew up at sea, most hands lost

The Bama's crew caught off guard
Our emotional shell began to crack
We feel the pain of mates now dead
Trying to understand that violent act

This tragic story with facts unknown
Our ship's scuttlebutt begins to grow
Surmising all possible scenarios
Searching for answers we don't know

Some claim they carried atomic bomb parts
Did they ignite, then explode
Did a Japanese sub or a small Kaiten
Torpedo the ship? Will we ever know?

When the Mighty Alabama no longer sails
None of its crew will ever forget
The day we let our invisible guard down
To salute the Indy's crew with respect

Battle Feelings
August 1945

Hauling up the anchor, our task force now underway
A sudden taste of salt water caught in an ocean spray

The halyard's flags changing, all ships sailed on time
An impressive show of power, Alabama falls in line

The Bama's bow plowing through high, angry waters
A tenacity of purpose sails forward, gives no quarters

Sailing into uncertain sphere where adversity lies in wait
Warships or air attacks, like a deadly spider and its bait

An uncontrollable heavy tremor within my stomach walls
My face decries my feelings standing straight, standing tall

A seasoned veteran of naval action, a leader to my crew
They draw upon my fortitude to lead them safely through

Ironically I'm held hostage to my duty and my pride
And all display of anguish, I am now impelled to hide

A quad leader's life is lonely as expectations run high
But after all I'm only human, not a hero, just a guy

The battle off Cape Engano in waters sent from Hell
We defeated the elusive Ozawa and Halsey rang his bell

Attacking Ocean Waves

The ocean sends rows of waves
Rising high to a misty maze

A sight to behold, a powerful force
Every wave stays on course

The tireless waves break and crest
Upon sandy beaches there they rest

There they rest but for a moment
Then quickly those waves ebb

Leaving a strange sandy pattern
Like a delicate spider's web

Sky Moods

An ocean sky once clear and pale blue
Now marred by clouds gray and white

Move cautiously by warm gulf streams
That gently aids them in their flight

Tropical depression off the coast
Clouds suddenly become an awesome sight

Clouds white and gray turn to black
And thunder and lightning increases fright

The aftermath of a tropical disturbance
Brings those dreary skies back to life

Dark storm clouds drift and fall apart
As if sliced with nature's knife

Melody of the Sea

Old sailors love the melody
Created by the waves and wind

The waves on rocks crash
And roar as the winds sing

There is nothing so sweet
To an old seaman's nautical ears

As the melody of the waves
As misty sprays wet his brow

And often bring tears to the eyes
Of the seafaring brave

Constant crashing on the rocks
Rushing tides with power to spare

Whistling wind like harmony
Sends string vibrations in the air

Underside View of a B-24L Liberator
The roll-up style bomb bay doors
were very distinctive to the Liberator.
1945

Mythical Tiger of Truk

One day a high flying altitude US Liberator
Boldly flew over Truk's harbor at noon
To Japan's Admiral Koga's complete dismay
And photographed the vast secret lagoon

The startled Admiral Koga pleaded with Japan
"I need more pilots and many more planes
My fleet has strength, but is badly under-manned."
The admiral's desperate plea was made in vain

A slight misty rain was now our blanket
At general quarters our ship did remain
As we watched our carriers launch a squadron
Of fast Hell Cats out of fast fighter planes

The US Navy then cracked Truk's defense
Our naval planes with aggressive skills
Caught Koga's planes on the runway
And our Hell Cats dove quickly for the kill

Two hundred Japanese planes, possibly more
Hurriedly started to take off from the ground
They were no match for our naval fighters
And they were destroyed as they were found

Now the scene shifts to the Imperial fleet
On the waters of the Pacific, two fleets will meet
The high floating clouds turned dark and dreary
And a chilling, cold feeling came with the rain

Anticipating a major sea naval battle
Now became our crew's anxious waiting game
A decisive sea battle the talk of the day
But Admiral Koga's fleet, in the dark, sailed away

A sad news report, Admiral Koga, the naval boss
Flying his seaplane, in a tropical storm, he was lost
Admiral Mitscher's Task Force has now set the tone
A crushing Japanese defeat by Operation Hailstone

The infamous mighty fortress, the Tiger of the East
But Truk's been exposed as a tiger without teeth

Hiroshima after 6 August, 1945
(National Archives and Records Administration)

The B-29 Superfortress bomber Enola Gay of USAAF lifted off from North Field of Tinian of the Mariana Islands 6 Aug. with the cargo code named "Little Boy". The crew was instructed that Hiroshima was to be their primary target; if Hiroshima could not be reached for any reason, Kokura or Nagasaki was to be chosen as alternate targets. They were accompanied by two B-29 bombers. One carried scientific instruments and the other carried photography equipment. Thirty minutes prior to reaching Hiroshima the bomb's safety devices were removed.

About 60 minutes before the American bombers reached Hiroshima, they were detected by Japanese radar. Air raid warnings were sounded in several cities, including Hiroshima, but when it was determined that there were only three bombers, thus it was likely to be only a reconnaissance mission, some of the cities lifted the alarm. At 0815 hours local time, "Little Boy" was released, 69% of the city destroyed.

By the end of 1945, Hiroshima's atomic bomb victims would increase to somewhere between 90,000 and 150,000.

Nagasaki after 9 August, 1945
(National Archives and Records Administration)

The second bombing was originally planned to be against the city of Kokura, which housed a major army arsenal, on 11 Aug. The schedule was moved up by two days to 9 Aug., however, due to predicted bad weather moving in on 10 Aug. The atomic bomb "Fat Man" was loaded onto the B-29 Superfortress bomber Bockscar. Two other B-29 bombers accompanied Bockscar. The Great Artiste carried scientific instruments and Big Stink with photography equipment. Unlike the Hiroshima attack, "Fat Man" was already armed when they took off due to the complexity of the Plutonium bomb.

Kokura was 70% clouded over. The target could not be visibly seen. Therefore it was on to Nagasaki. One of the most important sea ports in southern Japan. It was a significant major war production center for warships, munitions, and other equipment.

At 1101 hours "Fat Man" was released. Somewhere between 40,000 and 70,000 people were immediately killed. By the end of 1945, death tolls directly related to "Fat Man" reached 80,000.

A Turning Point

A sailor's decision
2 September, 1945

The morning of 2 September, 1945 felt like any other morning on the USS Alabama, except this was the day the peace treaty with Japan will be signed aboard the USS Missouri. I stepped onto the main deck and noticed the morning fog had started to rise. The scene over the aft fantail was breathtaking: Mount Fujiyama seemed to be suspended in the air. I had read books on the Shinto religion and imagined how the Kami would dance around this mountain top or perhaps their first god-like emperor, Jimmu Tenno, would appear on the mountain.

Even though this was an historic day in history, my mind was filled with doubts as to the direction my life was heading. I had served in the navy for nearly four years. I had become accustomed to the ways of sea life. I also had learned more about myself as a sailor in war time and now realized I had more abilities than I knew as a civilian. I had a completely different outlook on life, had found myself and now realized that I could rise as high as I wanted with my effort. The navy actually intensified my quest for knowledge. It also taught me to face life one day at a time. But did I really want to be discharged? I was not sure, but I had another emotion that made me long to see my family in Rhode Island.

Although the Missouri is anchored close to our ship, we still are a long way from the actual viewing scene. I wonder if this peace treaty will actually achieve peace, and will this mean the end of the rapacious efforts of the Imperialist nations to dominate the world? They believed World War I would end all future wars, but they still happen. I have a feeling that this peace treaty will not stop other nations from declaring war.

Admiral Conrad E. L. Helfrich
Signing the Japanese surrender document
on behalf of the Netherlands
aboard the USS Missouri.
2 September, 1945

General Douglas MacArthur
Stands beside him

USS Missouri
Anchored in Tokyo Bay
2 September, 1945

Our Given Rights
Written on the fantail of the USS Alabama
during the signing.

The forefathers of our country
Composed the precious Bill of Rights
Handed down through generations
For this gift we now must fight

For many centuries other countries
Have envied our Bill of Rights
But the benefactors of our constitution
Were not always ready for a fight

Whenever a catastrophe befalls us
And our safety suddenly goes astray
Many frightened and foolish people
Willingly give their rights away

Fear's a deadly, consuming poison
That clouds judgment in our minds
Accepting protection by trading their rights
A type of loss you never find

In time of war or terrorists attack
The perpetrators are heard to say
"Surrender your forefather's rights"
And the fearful people say "Okay"

Fear in itself is the problem
A tool often used by the powers that be
Trading your rights for your safety
They promise to set you free

For every loss because of fear
Because of the courage that we lack
Regardless of promises that were made
You'll not ever get them back

Every war since colonial times
Brave Americans are ready to fight
For our country's precious freedom
And our forefather's Bill of Rights

Many have suffered, many have died
To preserve the rights we've gained
To let them die because of our fears
Means their sacrifices were in vain

Remembering Washington, Patrick Henry
Ben Franklin and Jefferson too
Fighting to preserve our Bill of Rights
Tell our forefathers, "We thank you"

Fleet Carrier USS Enterprise

With wartime camouflage under way
with F6F Hellcats and SB2C Helldivers
on her deck, 1944.

Tokyo Bay

September 1945

Those long-awaited words the ship's PA system rendered
"At long last the war is over, Imperial Japan has surrendered"

The Alabama's crew again in the enemy's waters cruise
With a well-deserved sigh of relief, they cheer the good news

But high in the sky off the coast of Imperial Japan
A lone Japanese Zero fighter with a Kamikaze in command

Circles our patrolling task force, as our tensions runs high
The fleet's entire anti-aircraft artillery paints a polka dot sky

The USS Enterprise carrier caught the pilot's attention
And destruction and death were the pilot's intention

A cloud of red fire, black smoke feels the fleet's tension
A dead Kamikaze, suicide pilot has completed his vengeance

At the end of August 1945, as the Revenge leads the way
Sailing straight towards Japan, dropping anchor in Sugamai Bay

Within the shadows of Mount Fuji, dense fog and mist so raw
We view the royal mountain, which leaves the crew in awe

There's a strange inner feeling, like a reverent feeling of fear
For many, many centuries, Japan's Mt. Fujama was very dear

I see a vision, many dancing Kamis, perhaps even Jimmu Tenno
They seem to float and dance around Fuji then fade and disappear

Every fleet ship with cautious moves, circling around the fleet
Armed sailors in motor crafts, prepared for whatever they meet

It is September the second in Forty-five, the temper of the times
Aboard the Admiral's flag ship Missouri, a peace accord is signed

God's Life Pattern

From the fantail of the Alabama, Tokyo Bay
September 1945

In God's great pattern of life
Mankind is but a thin thread

Traveling God's earth as a voyeur
From man's birth until he's dead

Each year reveals a new experience
Searching for power to understand

Mankind's a body of human emotions
A woven pattern in God's great plan

Mankind, lost in anger and confusion
Seeking the enlightenment of understanding

While walking between good and evil
Relies on faith and God's blessing

Through faith man finds self-esteem
Avoiding the pitfalls of negativity

A question asked but misunderstood
My confusing role in life's reality

Many souls pray for self-empowerment
To recognize their earthly role

The desperate cries of those left behind
Blame God for their missed goal

Another Day

The scarlet sky with streams of yellow
Calm ocean scene at time of dawn

Rolling waves move in their gentle roll
As nature views a new day born

Migrating geese polka dot the sky
As white seagulls gliding suddenly dive

Small crabs cling desperately to rocks
The smell, the sounds, the air is now alive

A majestic swan and swimming gray ducks
Search for food along the watery way

Deep footprints made in soft beach sand
Those deep impressions will never stay

Leaping Neutrons
1945

The peaceful stillness of the night
Lost in sleep and free from fright

Flashing lightning erodes the darkness
Crashing thunder climaxes the contest

Thoughts of sleep now fade away
Then leaping up my legs obey

Hearts of the dogs begin to race
Back and forth they continue to pace

Rotating neutrons a merry-go-round
One thrown loose towards the ground

Deadly fork lightning neutrons streak
Following neutrons' earthbound leap

Tragedy's Impact
1945

I walk in darkness with mental anguish
A confused, frustrated, mind

An unforeseen demise, a loved one
An understanding I cannot find

The impact of this tragic moment
Lost in a maze of emotional grief

Fighting anger and self pity
Searching desperately for relief

Praying for the ability, capacity
To find the meaning of my loss

Silently I now often wonder
Will my mind find life's course

Unconsciously, I find I'm reaching
This road to reason is too hard

I need the help of friends in sorrow
I need the guidance of my God

Battleship USS Alabama (BB-60)
Arriving at San Francisco, California, United States
October 1945

The trip back to Long Beach, California seemed mild compared to the journey into harm's way. The crew is all hyped up about how many points they have towards being discharged. I have decided to be discharged when my point level allows that transition. I'll try civilian life for a while and if I don't see a satisfying future, I'll reenlist and make the navy my career.

Nearly four years of my youth was spent in the service of my country. My home for that length of time was the US Navy. Now, after becoming acclimated to service life, I was heading towards the world of civilian life. The first step in my return to a new future would be a long boring ride in a box car, made into sleeping quarters. It would take me from the West Coast to the East Coast for a discharge ceremony. The Fargo Building in Boston, Massachusetts was filled with returning veterans from the Pacific Coast area. We were ready to enter the life of the civilians. One overnight stay at the determent center, a discharge paper, and we once again became part of the Free Men Society. No more curfews, no more chow lines, and no more inspections.

John E. O'Hara, Gun Captain
40 MM Antiaircraft Quad 8
Pictured at discharge, late October 1945
(Courtesy of John E. O'Hara)

Point Judith
1945

A peninsula, like a long, thin index finger
Point Judith dips into the Atlantic Ocean
A Coastguard station's tall lighthouse
Overlooks the angry waves in motion

I love to sit and watch the white caps
As they roll in cadence far at sea
Waves break in synchronizing rhythm
Dancing to King Neptune's rhapsody

Eastern arms of the breakwalls
Break large waves that leap, then crash
Scaring those unsuspecting vacationers
With a large, cold, wet salt water bath

There are times the heavy fog rolls in
The lighthouse foghorn begins to mourn
With its low, loud monopolistic sound
That warns all ships of the danger zone

Point Judith's waters have a harbor of refuge
Three long, protective breakwall arms
Standing like sentinels, always standing strong
Keeping all ships and boats safe from harm

The Atlantic flood tides with fast rolling waves
Cover every beach with snow white beads
The Atlantic's ebbing tides slowly retreat
Leaving a long trail of green sea weeds

Seven

1946

John Home from the War
And happy to see his brother Robert and sister Irene
(Courtesy of John E. O'Hara)

John kept a notebook while he was in the Navy. Even though he was home in 1946 he continued rewriting his stories into rhyme. Some were his experiences and some stories were told to him by long time seamen.

The Story of the Three Davids

Battle of the Philippines
Written January 1946

Halsey's Third Fleet carrier
Planes raining torpedoes and bombs
Forced the Sho-Gun One Goliath fleet
To retreat to the East and flee

Kurita's damaged Central Force
Turns about and sails west
With desperate, loyal determination
To complete their quest

The sea looked deceptively smooth
Kincaid's fleet in darkness
The air filled with apprehension
Kurita's force, the Imperial best

A dreary melancholy day, a hazy sun
On the horizon masts appear
Destroyers, converted flat tops
Suddenly a squall, all mast disappear

Taffy 3 under a heavy barrage
Three guarding destroyers counterattack
The Johnston, Hoel, and Heerman
The courageous David torpedo pack

Admiral Sprague, a hard decision
"Into the open-draw Admiral Kurita"
Three Davids attack
The heavy cruisers quickly launching ten torpedoes

The Johnston's Cherokee captain
"Attack the Kumano with torpedoes"
Kurits' a heavy cruiser takes a direct hit
Enemy responds with all they can throw

The Hoel attacked two heavy cruisers
Kurita's battleship joins the uneven fight
A shell destroys Hoel's main engine
And jammed Hoel's rudder hard right

A Jap battleship chases the Heerman
But this spunky David pressed the attack
With decks covered in shell fragments
The spunky Heerman still fought back

Four Imperial cruisers release a barrage
At carriers Gambier and Kalinin Bay
The crippled Johnston attacks the cruisers
As two converted carriers slip away

Her bridge destroyed, engine damaged
One mount firing, fought back instead
Aggressive Johnston, a watery grave
141 crewmen survived but 186 were dead

A sister ship, the destroyer Hoel
Crippled by Kurita's heavy cruisers shells
Hoel kept firing at the enemy cruisers
Until at last, her final bell

Kurita's three cruisers and two battleships
Were damaged, withdrew without a sound
The admiral feared the Third Fleet was near
Turned his Central Fleet around

Their superior numbers against Taffy 3
The weakest force they could not defeat
But facing Halsey's fast Third Fleet
Admiral Kurita's final choice was retreat

The incredible story of three destroyers
Through naval history will always last
Although badly outnumbered
The courageous Three Davids were never outclassed

A Clash of Egos
January 1946

Two great men of stature
Possessing very strong wills
They're unmovable forces
With strong warriors' minds

Their strong, stubborn stances
And big egos that build
They are two military giants
Now within their time

General Douglas MacArthur
A tall, proud army man
A military leader with attitude
And tone so brash

Admiral William "Bull" Halsey
Always in command
Their strong, stubborn egos
Someday will clash

Admiral Mitscher's fifth fleet
Now Halsey's third
Sailed into Leyte Gulf
Via a very violent typhoon

His fleet whipped by the Cobra, in sea so weird
The Cobra's dance of destruction, to Neptune's tune

General MacArthur, the high command in charge
"Retake the Philippines, an amphibious assault"

But the Imperial Naval Admiral Toyota vows
"Bring the assault landings to a complete halt"

Prelude to the last great Philippine naval battle
Admiral Toyota's 71 ships now divided by three

Admiral Kurita is in the San Bernardino Straits
Admirals Nichimura and Shima sail into Surigao Sea

Trickery, deceit that is sailing in the straits
"It's Admiral Ozawa, no wait, that's a mistake

It's Admiral Kurita and he's now under way"
MacArthur and Halsey, in the Gulf you must stay

Off Cape Engano, Admiral Ozawa's fleet sighted
Sailing north east, "Bull" Halsey becomes excited

An unprecedented move, Halsey's Fleet in pursuit
Task Force 38, ready to fight, changes its route

Admiral Ozawa, the decoy, playing hide and seek
Successfully makes "Bull" Halsey's curiosity peak

An angry determined Halsey aborted his orders
Leaving a mad, furious MacArthur, for northern waters

The scene of the greatest naval battle in history
But for the Japanese Naval Fleet, a crushing defeat

As for those two men of stature and strong wills
Their two giant, super egos, they finally did meet

The Wisdom of God

January 1946

Mankind has always wondered about life's tragedies
The storms, the sickness and their loved one's death

They blame God in Heaven for not protecting them
In their anger and sorrow putting God to the test

"Please God in Heaven, You must always protect us
From all the evils and suffering of our daily lives

You place the ocean clams in a protective shell
That shields them from all harm and the ocean strife"

Then God answered, "The ocean clams in their shells
In their confines, protective safety they safely lie

But remember this, when those strong shells are opened
Every poor, well-protected clam will then die"

The Heavenly Father's speaking wisdom to His subjects
"I have no doubt that you really believe that I am wrong

But if I were to shelter and protect all of mankind
Like those ocean clams, you would never become strong"

The Question
January 1946

From now and until forever
A quizzical question will be asked

"Did "Bull" Halsey's sudden departure"
In reality actually desert Taffy 3

Admiral Ozawa, Halsey's nemesis
The decoy who drew him away

Ozara lost his fleet and air force
In Halsey's victory that fateful day

General MacArthur said in a rage
"I ordered him off Leyte to stay"

Halsey took over command
He demolished Ozawa, did not disobey

Leyte Commander MacArthur said
A Halsey court marshal's the fix

But Washington then disagreed
Halsey is under Admiral Nimitz

The Mystical Sea Raider

Story from an old time British sailor
1946

When British navy veterans
Chat over warm ale
The number one war topic
That will always prevail

The mystical Scharnhorst
That sailed like a ghost
Along the cold North Cape
Where she often sailed

Constantly tracking convoys
Like a bloodhound
The mysterious raider
Who controlled the North Sea

This fabulous cruiser
With a proud sense of pride
Always tormented and traumatized
The British Crown

Sailing proudly under the flag
Of her German homeland
Two fast and armed sea raiders
Were getting under way

Sailing north past Iceland
Through the Denmark Straits
They were searching carefully
For those unsuspecting prey

They boldly sailed into the cold
Unforgiving waters
The masts of an allied convoy
In the distance appeared

The crew of the raiders
Ordered their crew to battle stations
Then directly towards unsuspecting prey
They silently steered

These two ghostly sea raiders
Attacked a British support ship
They fired and sank a British carrier
The HMS Glorious

The shocking news soon reached
The British Home Fleet
The reputation of the mystical
Sea raider became notorious

They hurriedly sailed back
Through the Denmark Straits
As the dawn revealed a large
Allied convoy's smokestacks

The overconfident battle
Sea raiders increased their knots
Then with the swiftness of a tiger
Began their strategic attack

The HMS Ramilles
An old and slow British battleship
Was guarding the flank
Of the allied merchant fleet

Her old turrets began to fire
Their 15 inch projectiles
And forced the startled sea raiders
To quickly retreat

The German Chancellor Hitler
Had a consuming fear
A surprise British amphibian
Invasion of Norway sent

The German Fleet
Boldly up the Dover Straits
A dangerous and foolhardy plan
His ships must obey

The mystical cruiser Scharnhorst
Led the German fleet
On a daring bold raid
Up through the English Channel

The German's unexpected maneuver
In England's backyard
Was more than the off-guard
Defenders could handle

The sea raider Scharnhorst
Now reversed her role
Constantly hunted by the
Persistent British Home Fleet

She quickly sailed northwest
Into heavy, stormy waters
A safe hidden haven
The German cruiser now seeks

The Scharnhorst turned southward
A complete surprise
The pursuing British used star shell
To lighten dark skies

The battleship Duke of York
Fired its projectiles
That destroyed the sea raider's radar
The ship's eyes

Then quickly four British destroyers
Launched torpedoes
Deep into the side of their
Tormenting German foe

The mystical German Raider
Tried desperately to be evasive
But her once-noted high speed
Is now only slow

The British concentration
Of constant heavy gun fire
Foiled the cruiser Scharnhorst's
Careful plan of escape

The British heavy guns
Shelled her into a blazing wreck
As the mystical sea raider
Exploded and sank at North Cape

The tragic end to a usually
Outstanding fighting ship
But no loud bands
No celebration for a job well done

Only a very black pall of smoke
Marked the ship's grave
At last the Mystical Scharnhorst
Had made her last run

A Leader's Path

August 1946

A leader's path throughout history
When wealth and power sets in

Compassion beguiles his victims
And his quest becomes a sin

The ever-powerful military resources
Of large invading nations

Soon force the weaker countries
Upon their knees in desperation

Exploding shells, death-dealing rockets
To just survive becomes so hard

While more powerful invaders called
Their action a mission for their God

Their hungry lust for fame and power
So many innocents die

Their greed for the victor's spoils
Leaves little time to cry

Eight

1947

Hypnotic Ocean Waves

The hypnotic magic of the sea
Rolling waves in chorus lines

Break upon the sandy beaches
Leaving traces of foamy brine

One small wave begins to grow
Rolling high as in a trance

Then like a giant water wall
The waves become an avalanche

Waves roll as white caps break
Swelling waves in cadence ride

Like orchestrated, trained dances
On sandy beaches, gently glide

The Ghosts of Bataan
This Story Told to John by a Survivor
From Pawtucket, Rhode Island, United States
January 1947

The allied troops on Bataan Peninsula
Their bitter ballad mocks
They often chant "Dug out MacArthur
Lies a-rockin' on the rock"

76,000 Allied and Filipinos
Under Japanese guards' cruel skills
Struggling to walk in the infamous Death March
Many were killed

Filipino officers and fighting men singled out
Security a threat
They were tied, knelled, killed by guards'
Swords and bayonets

The Allied POWs suffered cruelty
From which there's no escape
Army angel nurses beaten, tortured
Then barbarically raped

Through confusion, errors,
Disease devastated troops of Bataan
Vinegar Joe's fighting forces
Displayed courage to the last man

Perpetrators of the surrender
Brought the troops to their knees
But it was malnutrition, malaria, beriberi
Not the Japanese

On that 60 miles
Now called the Road of Death
Pacific warm winds blow
Across this cursed land

It's said you can feel each victim's
Sadly dying breath
Drifting over the Philippine land
Known as Bataan

The horrific abuses of prisoners
On an island called Palauan
Prisoners in an air raid shed
Cremated alive to the last man

The loading of Allied prisoners
On those ships sent from Hell
A dark, filthy hole with little food
Their destination Japan

The Allied sick and wounded
Lay prone in an open trench
Soaked with gasoline by guards
The Japanese sealed their fate

Much too weak to rise,
They began to gag from the strong stench
The Japanese barbaric cruelty
And atrocities increase the hate

American Soldiers Resting During
The Bataan Death March
May 1942

The Bataan Death March was a sixty mile march.
It was forced upon captured Filipino and American Soldiers.
Between 7,000 and 10,000 Filipinos died on the march
and 2,330 American Soldiers died also.

Nine

John Today

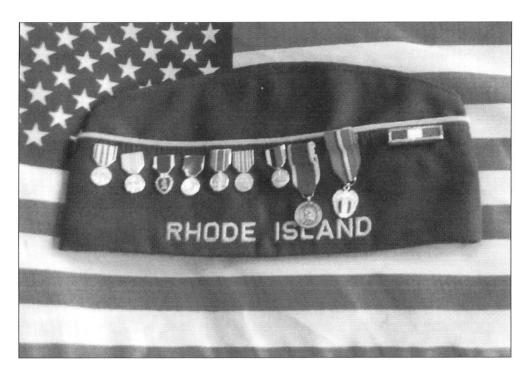

John is very proud of this hat with all his medals as he very well should be. He brushed death and escaped death a number of times while serving his country. When Shirley, his only love, passed away in 2004, he promised her he would dedicate the rest of his life volunteering and educating our young people about World War II; about the sacrifices he and so many more like him made so they could have the freedom they enjoy today. The medals are identified on the following page.

John E. O'Hara
The medals on his hat are listed L-R

Europe-Africa-Middle East WW II Medal
(1 Bronze Battle Star)

Asiatic-Pacific Camp Medal WW II
(2 Silver Stars)

Purple Heart

Navy WW II Good Conduct Medal

WW II Victory Medal

American Campaign Medal

WW II Occupation Medal Navy

Philippine (SHPI) Presidential Citation
Philippine Presidential Unit Citation Medal

Philippine Liberation Medal WW II

Philippine (SHPI) Presidential Unit Citation Bar

John E. O'Hara
World War II – Gun Captain

The Myths of War

One of the biggest myths of war was created by the entertainment industry when they portrayed servicemen as cheerleaders when they finished a battle. The truth is we were too busy doing our job and trying to stay alive. We had no time to stand up and cheer whenever an enemy plane was shot down or an enemy ship was sunk.

The one thing they never mentioned was the stress that consumed our bodies after the battle was over. Some men played cards, some played music and others just lay in their bunks trying to unwind.

I discovered, after landing in North Africa and having my ship sunk by German torpedoes, that writing about the action in a poetic style would unwind my tension. I found that when I wrote a poem in verses like Poe, Longfellow and Stevenson, I would have to fully concentrate on each verse and when I finished a poem, I felt relaxed and could fall asleep.

I wrote poems after every battle and today I have over 50 poems about World War II. I never intended to be classified as a poet, just someone who put in words what I was feeling at the time.

The moment the PA system released the words, "All Hands – Man Your Stations, Bogies Sighted," we would jump out of bed in the darkened compartment, quickly get dressed and rush to our 40 MM gun quads. Your mind's half awake. Your body reacts like a robot and your heart has dropped below your stomach (or so it seems) and all is in silence.

John E. O'Hara
Judge Advocate – Life Member
Disabled American Veterans

He is the go between for the local
Post to the National Organization
of the Veterans of Foreign Wars

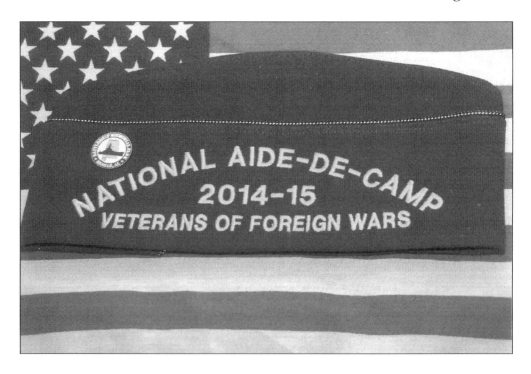

John is invited every year to be the flag bearer
at the Carol Stuart Pre-school.
2014

Kelly-Gazzerro, VFW Post 2812
Community Service Outreach Program

World War II veteran John E. O'Hara addressed the Narragansett
Junior Class during an assembly in March 2014

The 93 year old Legislative officer related his life during the war,
from boot camp to the peace signing in Tokyo Bay on 2 September, 1945

A young Naval officer, Steve Decar,
raised his glass during a dinner meeting and gave this toast:

**"My country – while having intercourse with foreign countries –
May she always be right – But right or wrong – My country"**

Students you live in the greatest country on this earth. Love and respect
your country. Always remember, right or wrong, it is still your country.

God Bless You and God Bless America

John E. O'Hara

To order any of Ray's books visit: www.raywolfbooks.com

 The Lost Villages of Scituate: In 1915, the general assembly appointed the Providence Water Supply Board to condemn 14,800 acres of land in rural Scituate. The hardworking people of the five villages were devastated. By December 1916, notices were delivered to the villagers stating that the homes and land they had owned for generations were....

 The Scituate Reservoir: In 1772, portions of Providence received water through a system of hollowed out logs. By 1869 the public voted in favor of introducing water into the city from the Pawtuxet River in Cranston. By 1900, it was clear more, and purer water was needed. A public law was approved on April 21, 1915, creating the Providence Water Supply...

 West Warwick: By 1912, the citizens of the western portion of Warwick had been talking about secession. They possessed all the mills on the Pawtuxet River and were largely democratic, while the eastern section was primarily republican. Finally in 1913, the Town of West Warwick was incorporated and became the youngest town in the state of Rhode...

 *Foster:* Originally incorporated as part of Scituate in 1731, became a separate community in 1781. The town was named in honor of Theodore Foster, a coauthor of the bill of incorporation. By 1820, the population topped out at 2,900 and then sharply declined. The population would not surpass the 1820 figures until 1975.

 *Pawtuxet Valley Villages:* Between 1806 and 1821, a dozen mills were built on the Pawtuxet River, shaping the economy of surrounding villages. The mills provided a livelihood for the villagers who settled in the valley and drew immigrants looking for a better life from Canada, Italy, Portugal, Sweden, and other faraway countries.

 *Coventry:* On August 21, 1741, the area west of what is now the Town of West Warwick was incorporated into the Township of Coventry. The railroad would traverse Coventry in the mid-1800s, providing the gristmills, sawmills, and farmers with a quicker way to send their goods to market and to receive supplies in return.

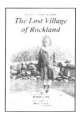

The Lost Village of Rockland is a book of photographs and documents with captions, featuring poems and tales by Helen O. Larson. She tells her story of growing up in the small New England Village of Rockland, in the Town of Scituate, Rhode Island in the early 1900s. She writes about having to suffer the agony of seeing her village vanish, one building at a time. Through her poetry, she tells stories....

Diary of Love Poems is the second book of the *Gramma Larson Remembers* series. It is a story of a love that began on a bus in 1956. It continued until her husband Ivar passed away 32 years later. However, Helen's love for Ivar did not end then. It carried on for another 17 years until she left to meet him on May 18, 2005. "As I go to sleep, and this poem closes my book to you, I will be dreaming…...

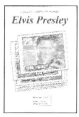

Elvis Presley is the third book in the *Gramma Larson Remembers* series. Her love for Elvis began in 1956 when she bought her son Raymond a portable record player with four 45 RPM records. One of the records was *Love Me Tender.* Through the years the boy born in a two room cottage in Tupelo, Mississippi rocked his way into her heart. The first poem Gramma wrote about him was; *A Super Star Was Born.*

Famous People, Family and Friends is the fourth book in the *Gramma Larson Remembers* series. She wrote her first poem in the summer of 1923 at the age of twelve. In her later years she picked up the handle of being called Gramma Larson. During her 82 years of writing rhymes, she wrote about many things. This book is broken down …...

Not part of the *Gramma Larson Remembers* series

Route 66 Today: Chicago, Il. to Needles, Ca. is a book of 223 color images with captions. The journey begins with breakfast at the famous Lou Mitchell's Restaurant in downtown Chicago. It then heads west to pass the Gemini Giant in Wilmington, Elvis in Braidwood, and Abraham Lincoln in Springfield before cruising into Missouri over....

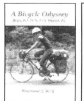

A Bicycle Odyssey: Hope, R.I. to N. Fort Meyers, Fl. began with a thought from my daughter, Donnalisa, as she spoke the words; "Wouldn't it be terrific if we all had ten speeds and we biked up to Uncle Paul's next year." You see my brother Paul, at the time, resided in Watertown, N.Y. Everyone thought we were crazy and would……

About the Author/Publisher

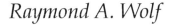

Raymond A. Wolf

Raymond A. Wolf is a lifelong resident of Hope, a small village in the southern part of the Town of Scituate, Rhode Island. He graduated from Scituate High School in 1961 and worked for AAA for 28 years. He retired, after 13 years as a manager of TJ Maxx, to pursue writing books full time. This is his fourteenth book. He belongs to six local historical societies and has become passionate about recording local history in the *Images of America* series by Arcadia Publishing. Much of this history is being lost for all time as the older folks are passing on. An equal passion he has is to include some of his mother's poetry in his books. His mom, Helen O. Larson, wrote 1,700 poems in her lifetime. His customers kept requesting when he was going to publish a book of her poems. However, he was unable to find a publisher to pick up on the idea. Hence, in 2014, he established Wolf Publishing. His first project was to create the *Gramma Larson Remembers* series. This series, featuring her poems, is his answer to his customer's request. He now has the freedom to publish what he wants and at a lower cost. He has even been able to hold the price on his full color books. Color is an option he never had before.

Made in the USA
Charleston, SC
12 September 2015